© Copyright 2016 - All rights rese

In no way is it legal to reproduce, duplicate, or transmit any part of this document in either electronic means or in printed format. Recording of this publication is strictly prohibited and any storage of this document is not allowed unless with written permission from the publisher. All rights reserved.

The information provided herein is stated to be truthful and consistent, in that any liability, in terms of inattention or otherwise, by any usage or abuse of any policies, processes, or directions contained within is the solitary and utter responsibility of the recipient reader. Under no circumstances will any legal responsibility or blame be held against the publisher for any reparation, damages, or monetary loss due to the information herein, either directly or indirectly.

Respective authors own all copyrights not held by the publisher.

Legal Notice:

This book is copyright protected. This is only for personal use. You cannot amend, distribute, sell, use, quote or paraphrase any part or the content within this book without the consent of the author or copyright owner. Legal action will be pursued if this is breached.

Disclaimer Notice:

Please note the information contained within this document is for educational and entertainment purposes only. Every attempt has been made to provide accurate, up to date and reliable complete information. No warranties of any kind are expressed or implied. Readers acknowledge that the author is not engaging in the rendering of legal, financial, medical or professional advice.

By reading this document, the reader agrees that under no circumstances are we responsible for any losses, direct or indirect, which are incurred as a result of the use of information contained in this document, including, but not limited to, —errors, omissions, or inaccuracies.

Table of Contents

Bitcoin: What You Need to Know About Bitcoin.

A Simple Guide for Beginners.

- INTRODUCTION
- CHAPTER 1- THE HISTORY OF BITCOIN
- CHAPTER 2: HOW BITCOIN WORKS?
- CHAPTER 3: GETTING STARTED WITH BITCOIN
- CHAPTER 4: HOW TO PROTECT YOURSELF AGAINST BITCOIN THEFT
- CHAPTER 5: HOW DOES BITCOIN MINING WORK?
- CHAPTER 6- THE FUTURE OF DIGITAL CURRENCY & BITCOIN
- Conclusion

INTRODUCTION

If you've chosen this book, chances are you've heard of Bitcoin, and you're probably curious to know what this unique thing is. Bitcoin has been gaining more and more attention as of late, and it's no wonder because more and more people see its benefits. Investors and financial institutions are ready to put their head in the game and reap the benefits of Bitcoins.

Not convinced? Before we go any further on what Bitcoins are and how you can use them, here are five people who have made millions through Bitcoin:

1- Charlie Shrem, CEO of BitInstant

Shream learned about Bitcoin in 2011 while a senior at Brooklyn College. He purchased several Bitcoins on Tradehill, a digital currency exchange similar to Mt.Gox. He made his first purchase of 500 Bitcoins for USD 3 and then made his millions when the value of BTC reached USD20.

2- Jered Kenna, CEO of Tradehill

Jered is one of Bitcoin's first investors, and his initial purchase of 5,000 coins was at 20 cents each. Jered once accidentally deleted 800 bitcoins when he wiped his computer clean back in 2010. But that's old news as Jered is now one of Bitcoin's central authorities.

3- Roger Ver, Investor

Ver was a former politician who ran for the California State Assembly in 2000. He ended up in prison and after ten months in jail, he relocated to Tokyo. Ver is one of the earliest evangelists for Bitcoin, infatuated with its promise of decentralization. Ver spent every waking moment learning about Bitcoin until he struck gold. He now gives away his Bitcoins for free.

4 & 5- Cameron And Tyler Winklevoss, Entrepreneurs

According to the New York Times, the Winklevoss, "have amassed since last summer what appears to be one of the single largest portfolios of the digital money". They currently own one percent of all Bitcoins in circulation. Their portfolio is valued at $11 million.

Now that you know a little bit about people who have made their share of the world's riches, this book will attempt to shed light on everything that is Bitcoin and help you navigate towards investing, successfully, in Bitcoin.

With that said, a little introduction is needed to give you a brief idea of what Bitcoin is and then we shall go into the specifics.

What is Bitcoin?

Bitcoin is part of the ever growing world of digital currently, and the first of its kind in a category called cryptocurrency. It's digital because it is created and held electronically- no prints, no dollars, no euros and no cents. No one controls it, yet, it is produced by people and businesses.

What Makes Bitcoin Different?

If you own Bitcoin, you technically can buy things electronically, so it is just like conventional dollars which are also bought and sold digitally.

But the difference between Bitcoin and traditional currencies is its unique characteristic, the fact that Bitcoin is decentralized. No financial institution or organization controls the Bitcoin network. This is one of the major attractions that draws people to invest in Bitcoin- no bank can monitor their money.

Who Created Bitcoin?

Satoshi Nakamoto is the name behind Bitcoin. He is a software developer that created an electronic payment system based on mathematical verification. Nakamoto's idea behind this was to produce a form of currency that was independent of central financial authority. What' more is that is can be transferred electronically, instantly and with very low transactions fees.

Who Prints Bitcoin?

No one prints Bitcoin. Central banks do not physically print them and are not accountable to the population, thus having its own set of trading rules. Bitcoin is produced digitally by a group of people in which anyone can participate. Bitcoin is mined, using computing power software via a distributed network.

This single system also processes transactions that are made through digital currency, thus making Bitcoin its own payment network.

The Bitcoin network runs on the Bitcoin protocol. This protocol constitutes the rules that ensure the way Bitcoin works. For example, only 21 million Bitcoins can be created by Bitcoin miners so that no one can churn out unlimited Bitcoins. But, these Bitcoins can be separated in smaller amounts, with the smallest divisible part being one hundred millionth of a Bitcoin which is called 'Satoshi' named after its founder.

What is Bitcoin Traded On?

Bitcoin is based on mathematical calculations, unlike conventional currency that is based on commodities, gold or silver.

Software programs follow a mathematical formula to produce Bitcoins and this mathematical formula is and open-source program, meaning it is freely available to anyone, and anyone can access it to make sure that it runs as it's supposed to.

Bitcoin Quick Facts:

Bitcoin is quickly gaining popularity in the world of trading. Here are some essential characteristics of Bitcoin that makes it the fastest-growing digital currency in our world:

1. It isn't controlled by any authority

In other words, we call it decentralized. Machines that mine bitcoins and process the transactions are part of the Bitcoin trading network and all these machines work together. In theory, there is no central authority that that determines monetary policies and causes a financial meltdown; neither can these financial bodies take away your bitcoins. Even if the system goes offline for whatever reason, money still keeps transacted.

2. It's easy to set up

By now, you know that opening a bank account takes a lot of effort. However, opening a Bitcoin account can be done in seconds, from the comfort of your own home. No questions asked and even better, no fees.

3. It's anyone's world

While anonymity can get some people worked up, it works to the best of advantages in Bitcoin. Bitcoin miners are allowed to have multiple Bitcoin addresses, and there is no verification of names or addresses or any other personal information.

4. It's Transparent

Sort of. While it is anonymous, Bitcoin does store each and every detail of every transaction in its network called a Blockchain. Think of the Blockchain as a large online version of a ledger book- it contains all and tells all. So this means anyone on the network can see how many bitcoins you have stored in your Bitcoin address- they just won't know it's you.

5. It Has Low Transaction Fees

Bitcoin doesn't charge exorbitant transfer fees when you conduct international transfers, unlike conventional banks.

6. It's Quick

Sending money anywhere in the world is easy and fast with Bitcoin. It's done within a few minutes; once the network processes the payment.

CHAPTER 1- THE HISTORY OF BITCOIN

Bitcoin is one of the most volatile digital currencies in our world currently. It is vastly influenced by a diverse range of dynamics and yet, up tp 100,000 bitcoin transactions takes place every day. This volume is expected to keep on growing because of the 'permission less innovation' which is the Blockchain, Bitcoin's own technology.

As more and more features are included in Bitcoin transactions such as Circle, Coinbase, and Bitnet, more and more places, businesses and people will continue with these transactions and mining Bitcoins.

In this Chapter, we will take a look back at how Bitcoin started and its major milestones as well as where it's headed in the future.

February 2007   The person credited as the founder of Bitcoin is Satoshi Nakamoto. He created this cryptocurrency and is said to be living in Japan. However, it is speculated that the name Nakamoto may be a collective pseudonym for more than one person working on this.

August 2008   Neal Kin, Vladimir Oksman, and Charles Bry make an interesting application for an encryption patent application. However, all three deny any relations to Satoshi Nakamoto. They register Bitcoin.org under anonymousspeech.com. This site enables anyone to register a domain anonymously and accepts Bitcoins as payments.

October 2008   Satoshi Nakamoto releases his white paper through metzdowd.com, revealing that he was indeed the mastermind behind the peer-to-peer version of an electronic cash transaction. Nakamoto also solves the problem of copying money, making this a significant milestone in enabling Bitcoin to grow legitimately.

October 2009   The New Liberty Standard establishes Bitcoin exchange rate, giving it an equivalent value with traditional currencies. So Bitcoin at US$1 is 1,309.03 BTC. This equation was done based on the cost of electricity used to run a computer that generated Bitcoins.

December 2009   Bitcoin Version 0.2 is released

March 2010   The first Bitcoin Market is established by dwdollar. Subsequently, an encryption patent application filed by Neal Kin, Vladimir Oksman and Charles Bry in August 2008 is finally published.

May 2010   The first real world Bitcoin transaction takes place by a programmer named Laslo Hanyecz in Florida. He pays 10,000 BTC and orders a pizza from Papa John's. At the time, the pizza was worth $25. Now the pizza is valued at $5.12 million, and on the 22nd of May, it became known asBitcoin Pizza Day.

July 2010   Bitcoin's value increases ten times from US$0.008/BTC to US$0.080/BTC.

August 2010   A loophole in the Bitcoin system is discovered and exploited resulting in the generation of 180 billion Bitcoins. This hack brings the value of the currency crashing.

October 2010   After the hack attack in August and subsequent vulnerability discoveries in Bitcoin's blockchain the following month, an inter-governmental group called the Financial Action Task Force develops and promotes policies to prevent money laundering and terrorist funding. They publish a report to warn others about the use of digital currencies.

November 2010   Bitcoin economy reaches $1 million. This surges the value of Bitcoins to $0.50/BTC.

December 2010   First Mobile transaction takes place

January 2011   Silk Road, an illicit Bitcoin marketplace is established, an untraceable way for drug dealing. Also called the eBay for drugs.

February 2011   Bitcoin reaches dollar-to-dollar equivalent of US$1.00/BTC to the US Dollar for the first time.

March 2011   The Bitcoin Market gets a major update- minimum trade sizes are reduced and trading is permitted 24 hours, seven days a week. Later on, a 1984 Celica Supra is traded for 3000 BTC by an Australian, making him the first person to trade a vehicle in exchange for Bitcoins. That same month, Bitcoin opens and becomes the first market to trade Bitcoins in British Pound Sterling (GBP). Next, Bitcoin Brazil is established, trading Brazilian Reals.

May 2011   TIME Magazine publishes an article on Bitcoin. The same month, Bitcoin reaches and passes parity with Euro and GBP.

July 2011   The largest Bitcoin theft is reported at 25,000 BTC. Wikileaks starts accepting Bitcoin

March 2012   Bitcoin Magazine launches

May 2012   Bitcoin Magazine goes into print editions

July 2012   Coinbase, a Bitcoin wallet, and platform are founded in San Francisco, California. Block 181919 becomes the largest block to-date with 1322 transactions.

October 2012   The Bitcoin Foundation is formed to drive a core development team to ensure protocols and oversee digital currency

January 2013   BitPay, a Bitcoin payment processing company, surpasses 10,000 transactions with zero cases of payment fraud reported.

March 2013   A major glitch causes a halt in transactions, resulting in a sharp sell-off and a 23 percent drop in value to USD$37. By the evening, the exchange rate recovers its value.

May 2013   Bitcoin on MtGox surpasses USD$100. That same month, the first Bitcoin ATM is unveiled in San Diego, California. Soon after, MtGox funds are seized by the United States Department of Homeland Security. Over USD2.9million is taken because it 'failed to register as a money transmitting business'.

July 2013   Tyler and Cameron Winklevoss establishes the Winklevoss Bitcoin Trust with the US Securities Exchange Commission. The Winklevoss twins say that the Exchange Traded Fund is a cost-effective and convenient means to gain exposure for investors with minimal credit risk.

August 2013   Bloomberg receives a Bitcoin ticker to enable Bloomberg employees to track the value of BTC under XBT currency.

October 2013   FBI shuts down operations of the infamous online drug dealing marketplace called Silk Road, seizing 3.6 million dollars of Bitcoins.

December 2013   The biggest heist in the history of Bitcoin takes place where 96,000 bitcoins are stolen from the Sheep Marketplace- an online drug store. Cyprus University becomes the first university to accept Bitcoin payments for tuition. Shopify and Virgin Galactic begins accepting Bitcoin. Bitcoin holds its first annual Black Friday.

January 2014   BitInstant CEO, Charlie Shrem is arrested over allegations of money laundering in connection with Silk Road. He eventually resigns from his position as vice chairman of Bitcoin Foundation.

February 2014   HMRC classifies Bitcoin as private money. It becomes the world's first and most progressive policy of Bitcoin.

June 2014   More than 29,000 bitcoins are auctioned off by the US government from the Silk Road raid. The closure and auction of Silk Road helped Bitcoin gain legitimacy and demonstrates that Bitcoin is not an easy way for criminals to avoid the law, even online.

July 2014   The European Banking Authority announces its stance on virtual currencies whereas the New York State Department of Financial Services releases the first draft of regulating virtual currencies, bringing the Bit License to reality.

December 2014   Microsoft accepts Bitcoins as payment options.

January 2015   The NYSE becomes a minority investor in Coinbase, aiming to bring in greater transparency, security, and confidence in Bitcoin.

March 2015   The UK Treasury calls for information on digital currency

Future Predictions

The development of Bitcoin seems to have a positive outlook, all of which moves towards greater legitimacy and the adoption of tighter regulations through large institutions. The New York's BitLicense became the first digital currency regulatory regime in the world and is expected to be in full force as time passes.

The European Central Bank and the European Banking Authority have also released reports detailing digital currencies and suggested regulations to further control Bitcoin's volatility and price fluctuations.

These reports mark progress towards the sustainable future of Bitcoin. With anti-money laundering laws and consumer protection and technical standardization for digital currency companies, this will encourage even more traditional financial services to adopt and engage with digital currency businesses, further accelerating the integration of blockchain technology.

CHAPTER 2: HOW BITCOIN WORKS?

The Basics of Buying and Selling with Bitcoins

Before we go into the specifics of how Bitcoin works, we will look at a few terms and details used in the Bitcoin world. In all honesty, you can get started with trading Bitcoins even without understanding the basics, but it's always good to read a little information.

To get started with Bitcoin, you need to have the Bitcoin wallet installed on your computer or smartphone. This app will generate your first Bitcoin address, and you can create more addresses whenever you need. Much like an email address, you can disclose your address to businesses or associates to send and receive payments.

Here are some key terms to know:

- The Blockchain

Think of the blockchain as an online shared public ledger on which the whole Bitcoin network relies on. Confirmed transactions are kept in the blockchain, and it allows Bitcoin wallets to calculate what the spendable balance is and verify new transactions by spending Bitcoins owned by the spender. Cryptography ensures the integrity and chronological order of the blockchain.

- Private Keys

Private keys are a secret data item that is stored in Bitcoin wallets. Also known as a seed, this is used to sign transactions and provide mathematical proof that they are from the owner of the wallet. A signature, unique to Bitcoin also prevents anyone else from altering the transaction once it has been issued. Transactions take about 10 minutes to be confirmed; it is broadcasted between users through a process called mining.

- Mining

Mining is the act of processing a transaction. It is a distributed consensus system that is used to authenticate pending transactions between users. These transactions are included into the blockchain. The mining process enforces a chronological order in the blockchain, thus increasing the protection of neutrality on the network. It also allows other computers to agree on the state of the system. Transactions must be filled into a block that fits in with the very strict cryptographic rule which will then be verified by the network and eventually confirmed.

How A Transaction Takes Place

- You establish your Bitcoin Address

- You want to make an online payment for Jewelry to a company called BitJewels using 5 bitcoins in your digital wallet

- BitJewel creates a new Bitcoin address and directs you to send your payment to that address

- A private key (only known to BitJewel) is created when the address is sent to you

- A public key (known to you and everyone else) is created at the same time

- You instruct your Bitcoin client (the software you first installed on your PC/mobile device) to transfer 5 Bitcoins to BitJewel's address from your wallet.

- Your Bitcoin client will then sign the transaction request electronically using the private key of the address from where you are transferring the Bitcoins to.

- Your transaction is broadcasted to the Bitcoin network

- Your transaction is verified in 10 minutes

- You have successfully transferred 5 Bitcoins from your address to the BitJewel address

Pros and Cons of Using Bitcoin

Like every other app, program or software, it is good to know the advantages and disadvantages of it.

ADVANTAGES

- It is the first cryptocurrency currently taking the world by storm and has managed to capture the public imagination.

- It has the head start over other competitors in the cryptocurrency world.

- Bitcoin's total issuance is limited to 21 million so it cannot be easily devalued due to the possibility of a massive influx of Bitcoins

- It is a decentralized currency, free from government interference and manipulation

- It has low transaction fees

DISADVANTAGES

- Bitcoins are extremely volatile

- Its volatility makes it hard to assess its real value and increases the risk of losses

- Its anonymity is vulnerable to be used for illegal and illicit activities such as drug dealing, gambling, terrorist funding and tax evasion

- It is susceptible to lose because Bitcoins exists primarily in digital form

Points to Ponder

While Bitcoin technology has made significant strides since it was unveiled in 2009, there is much improvement that needs to be done for this type of digital currency. The evolution, security, and openness of business and consumers of accepting it as a form of payment will greatly determine the success of Bitcoin in years to come. Efforts made by financial bodies as well as large corporations will be an integral part of Bitcoin's success as becoming a global financing system or just as a niche digital currency player.

The Basics of Trading in Bitcoin

One of the simplest ways to start trading and investing in Bitcoin is just to go online and buy some!

There are many established firms in the US and abroad that are involved in buying and selling Bitcoins, making it very easy for novice traders and the Average Joes and Jane's to buy them.

Coinbase is one of the most popular Bitcoin businesses on the Bitcoin network. This company sells Bitcoins to customers, but at a markup rate which is usually at 1% more than the current market price.

Coinbase has an option to link your bank account conveniently to your Coinbase Wallet, making transactions easy. With Coinbase, you are buying and selling directly from the firm.

BitStamp offers a more traditional Bitcoin exchange where you trade with other users and not with the company. Liquidity is higher here, and the fees begin at 0.5% and go as low as 0.2%.

Other Ways to Purchase Bitcoins

Another popular way to buy Bitcoins offline is through a website called Local Bitcoins. This site matches potential buyers with sellers- think of it as Tinder for Bitcoins. A seller's Bitcoins are locked in the escrow, and the seller can only release it directly to a buyer.

If you purchase Bitcoins offline, then be mindful that you are dealing with a total stranger so put in place precautions such as meeting during the daytime in a public place and do bring a friend.

The Basics of Investing in Bitcoin

Bitcoins are becoming an increasingly popular way to invest and gain enormous payoffs. This is the reason why it has a huge following of supporters. However, just like every other form of investing, Bitcoins are also a chance and luck gamble.

Bitcoin can be thought of as half technology and half money. You can choose to own it by managing the technology yourself or having someone else manage it for you.

Here are more tips on how to buy, invest as well as store Bitcoins and also extra guidance on how to choose between these three methods.

For the Tech-Savvy Investor

Since the Bitcoin Core launch in 2009, many other new apps have been created but like the original software, most of these new apps also have a 'user-controlled wallets' interface. These types of wallets enable users to manage their own private keys.

However, the latest services include 'hosted wallets' which takes care of these private keys for the users.

Tech savvy investors are encouraged to use user-controlled wallets as it offers much greater privacy without the need of any third party intrusion. The good news is that you have full control over your money. The not so good news is that you could lose your private keys if your computer is hacked. These keys could also be stolen if your computer breaks down. If you have no other records of your keys, you will not have access to your transactions and wallets.

These wallets come in desktop, mobile or web apps and these apps come in two forms- full node and simplified payment verification (SPV).

Full Node: This means that the full blockchain will be loaded, and the entire record of each and every transaction ever made in

Bitcoin will be stored in your computer. Take note that the current file capacity is 51,000 MB and this program typically takes a couple of days to load even on high internet speed. It will also take up a lot of memory on your hardware. Bitcoin and Bitseed are such applications.

Simplified Payment Verification: a lightweight wallet. In other words is much easier to use to pay for items especially if you are always out and about. Mycelium is one type of user-controlled mobile wallet.

For A More User-Friendly Experience

Hosted wallets provide a much user-friendly experience. These wallets are hosted by a third party, and it takes care of your private keys. It also offers user experience via the web and mobile app, much like your online bank accounts.

Third Party accounts are also vulnerable to hackings and sometimes, there is a possibility of withholding your funds. With some hosted wallets, you also end up giving up your ability to access your Bitcoin and view or verify it on the blockchain.

For example, if you have a Coinbase wallet, and you have sent in payment to a recipient of another Coinbase wallet, you may not be able to view this on the public blockchain.

Experts recommend that you choose a service that offers a two-factor authentication method. Most online banks do this as well, where a code is sent to your mobile phone to access the account.

For Those Concerned About Security

Apparently, there are wallets for every kind of investor. If you have this immense fear of losing your Bitcoins in some form or other, don't fret! There are options for maximum security. Some people don't trust themselves in keeping their private keys safe, and they also do not want to give complete control to third party wallets. If this applies to you, you can go for the hybrid option. The hybrid option is a company that offers multi-signature transactions. These transactions allow you not to hold your keys yourself or give it entirely to a company.

Unlike other transactions that only allows one private key to authorize, the hybrid wallet allows several keys that are associated with the address, (typically a minimum of 2 to a maximum of 5 keys) to be used to sign in before the money can be transferred to the recipient address.

This is similar to how banks require at least three signatures for company checks of a certain amount of money in order for it to be valid. One such hybrid wallet is by BitGo.

Another highly secure way to store your Bitcoins would be in a vault, but this would mean you need to trust a third party. It's the same thing as storing your money in a bank (the third party) as opposed to underneath your mattress. Xapo provides this storage services for investors- so you have high security and at the same time, you will be able to access your funds anywhere, anytime.

Hardware Wallet

Hardware wallets are a good idea as well if you want to retain control of your keys, but do not want them to be available on the internet due to hacking or malware issues. The hardware wallet is a USB stick sort of device specifically built to hold your private & public Bitcoin keys. Think of this device the same way you would use a USB stick- it can be plugged into any computer to conduct transactions. Private keys are not revealed on the computer being used to make the transactions, thus preventing hackers or malware from accessing this device. Hardware wallets to consider are the LedgerWallet, Trezor, and KeepKey.

How can you get your hands on Bitcoin?

User controlled wallets are the easiest and are a way of obtaining Bitcoins such as through Coinbase, Fitbit, Circle, and Gemini. These services also offer you the option of linking your wallets to your bank account.

You can also buy Bitcoins through Bitcoin ATMs or a local exchange that offers Bitcoins such as Local Bitcoins or Mycelium Local Trader.

Hosted wallets also make it easy for investors to obtain Bitcoins and it also connects you to your online banking system, making it easy for you to purchase bitcoins through ACH, check or wire transfer.

Investing with Bitcoin Investment Trust (GBTC)

If you don't plan on spending your Bitcoins to purchase products, you can invest them through GBTC. GBTC is a trust that provides investors the Bitcoin exposure but in a traditional security. GBTC is modeled after SPDR Gold Shares ETF, and it is a publicly traded security that is invested in Bitcoin. Each share of the GBTC is valued at one-tenth of a Bitcoin.

CHAPTER 3: GETTING STARTED WITH BITCOIN

Now that you have an idea of the terms of Bitcoin, different wallets, security features and so on, it's time to look at a step-by-step guide in helping novice Bitcoiners in sending, receiving and investing their Bitcoins.

Getting started with Bitcoin

This chapter is perfect for those of you who want to test the waters trading with Bitcoin.

Step 1- Install your digital wallet

First, head to Bitcoin.org. As a new user, you need to install a digital wallet on your PC, MAC or smartphone (https://bitcoin.org/en/choose-your-wallet). This wallet is free and open-source software that will generate your first and future Bitcoin addresses. There are three types of wallets that you can choose from:

1. A software wallet that is installed on your PC

2. A mobile wallet installed on your mobile device

3. A web wallet located on the website of the service provider hosting the bitcoins

Each time an address is created, Bitcoin employs key encryption techniques for maximum security. This is a key pair that includes a public key and a private key that constitutes a set of unique letters and numbers.

Every address has its own Bitcoin balance so users just need to obtain many Bitcoins that will be held in one of the addresses in the Bitcoin wallet. Bitcoins can be obtained many ways such as purchasing them from a Bitcoin currency exchange such as MtGox or Bitstamp, or users can also use services such as BitInstant that allows funds transactions to occur between Bitcoin exchanges.

To increase privacy and security, Bitcoin experts suggest creating new addresses for each transaction because not all Bitcoin transactions will be stored publicly and permanently on the Bitcoin network.

Step 2- Test Your New Bitcoin Wallet

You can test your new Bitcoin wallet by going to www.dailybitcoins.org. This page allows you to paste your Bitcoin address to check it. Uncheck 'Delay payment to minimize transactions fees'- this is just to trick people. Once you have entered the captcha code, click send. Wait 10 minutes then open your Bitcoin Wallet software. At the Transactions tab, you should be able to see a transaction of 0.00001 bitcoins. This means you have gained a few Bitcoins.

Step 3- Mining

Mining is the act of online transactions through Bitcoin. As described in earlier chapters, mining can only be done when you have an address and have Bitcoins and when a service or company sends you an address for you to make a payment. Mining is a way of verifying Bitcoin transactions conducted by other people in return for new bitcoins. There are two types of mining:

Solo- Solo mining is done on your own. However, using the computer hardware of an average Joe, it would take your years to reach a substantial amount of Bitcoins. So if you get 50 Bitcoins, you get about USD500. But this takes such a long time, which is why:

Pool- this is a more widespread and common mining method. It involves a user signing up for an account with any Bitcoin service provider. These companies group together mining efforts of lots of people's computers using their software and hardware. Each person pooled will get a small number of bitcoins. This is the way to go for an individual with a modest computer.

Step 4- Setting up a Mining Account

Find a mining pool that you find easy to use. For this example, we will use BitMinter. BitMinter is by far the easiest to use and it also comes with its own software. To set up your mining account, go to bitminter.com/login. Next, choose the account you want to link with BitMinter and use the login details of your account. Like many accounts today, there is an existing service called an OpenID which conveniently allows you to log into an already-existing account to reduce the need to remember a new password. Think of how you can log into your Pinterest or Instagram account using your Facebook account.

Set your email address as well as your auto cast out threshold to a sensible amount. A good figure would be 1 BTC (approximately USD10). Whenever you mine 1 BTC, you will receive it into your Bitcoin wallet. Determine your "pay to address". This is the address that all your Bitcoins will be sent.

Step 5- Setting Workers

For each computer connected to the BitMinter server, you need to have a worker. Each computer has a different worker sent to the BitMinter server, and it will not have any issues transmitting and receiving mining work. At the BitMinter website, go over to 'My Account' at the top page then click on Workers. You can create your Worker by giving a specific name such as My Laptop or My Pad. Then create a password for it. Click Add.

Step 6- Setting up a Miner

At the BitMinter homepage, click on the 'Engine Start' button which will download a Java Web starter and the actual program to install it. Next time you want to start the program, use this file instead. Link your worker with the software with the username you created your BitMinter account with. Besides the 'Engine Start' button, link it with the devices you want to use. Usually, you should only focus on running devices that give you 25Mhps or above. You also want to check your automated settings. Automated devices are devices that you can set a start time on them, so they automatically turn on when the software starts up.

Step 7- Mining Time!

Now let your computer run to mine Bitcoins. Experts recommend running your computer during the night so that it can double the amount of money you make.

Step 8- Spending & Investing your Bitcoins

You can spend your hard-mined Bitcoins by trading it for PayPal money, investing it at a MtGox Bitcoin Exchange, buying merchandise or services like Expedia, Dell, Wordpress.com, Subway, Zappos and Whole Foods. MtGox is the most common site to trade your Bitcoins for any national currency. Money is transacted to your Paypal account or any other accepted currency transfer service.

Step 9- Sending your Bitcoins to Someone

Sending Bitcoins must be done with another person who has a Bitcoin address. All you need to do is copy the particular address, open your Bitcoin wallet, click on 'Send Coins' enter the address and click on 'Pay'.

CHAPTER 4: HOW TO PROTECT YOURSELF AGAINST BITCOIN THEFT

Bitcoin's high-end security features are one of the main attractions in the realm of digital currency. Its main outstanding feature is the untraceable individual identifying information- which is why it is a boon for illegal activities. However, recent policies and measures put into place have curbed these activities, giving investors higher assurance, reliability, and security.

Each Bitcoin transaction is also publicly recorded but is not irreversible. Your private keys to your wallet alongside your personal identifying information are kept highly encrypted and secret.

Ironically, these factors that make Bitcoin so secure are also the factors that contribute to extensive attempts for hacking.

Anonymity of Bitcoin

Bitcoin's public feature for transactions minimizes fraud from happening. On the other hand, the anonymity of the currency is a major desirability. Transactions via Bitcoin are harder to trace to its original source, thus maintaining an individuals' privacy online.

Bitcoin Wallet Security

One of the main arguments for Bitcoin security has little to do with the safety of Bitcoin transactions. Rather, it has more to do with Bitcoin wallets as they are not as safe as can be. Your Bitcoins are as safe as the wallets it is kept in. Bitcoins can be stolen- just like traditional currency in your wallet. The difference is, hackers or online thieves need to be more tech savvy to 'grab' a wallet online than on the street.

Viruses and Malware

Viruses and malware exist anywhere on the internet. Hackers use these tools to break a code, hack into drives, manipulate a system and alter algorithms. In the Bitcoin world, hackers use these elements to gain access to private keys and enable money transfer to their own wallets. With Bitcoin, once the money has been transferred, there's pretty much nothing you can do about it because Bitcoin transactions are irreversible.

With all of these security threats, how can the future of digital currency and cryptocurrencies evolve over time?

Bitcoin is by far the most successful form of cryptocurrency in our world today. This network has demonstrated a lot of advantages, especially in security terms since its early days. Of course, there were weaknesses too that thankfully, were discovered and rectified.

One of the biggest incidents of theft reported on Bitcoin transactions was the Bitstamp hack in which 19,000 BTC were stolen when a loophole was discovered by hackers and quickly manipulated. The loss was at USD 5 million.

After Bitstamp, there were several other hacking incidents. Not only that, there was the Silk Road scandal which sort of jeopardized Bitcoin's image as a currency trader. The question is, does this put Bitcoin's future in peril?

Irreversible Transactions

There is no middle man when it comes to Bitcoin transactions, thus giving no room for an intermediary to come and reverse the transactions. The only way to return a payment is if the recipient of the payment returns it to the sender.

Bitcoins that are stolen retain their value and usability. However, several measures have to be taken to track stolen coins. These measures have not yet been implemented. Because Bitcoin transactions are public (personal information is private), it makes it even more important to increase one's privacy for every virtual wallet they have.

Taking all the issues stated above into account, we can now speak a little bit more about the measures that an individual can take to heighten the security when payments are made, protecting your identity and also your digital wallets from any potential theft.

Tip 1- Using a resourceful Bitcoin client

You should use a Bitcoin client that allows you to change or create a new address for each transaction you make. Why the hassle? This is to create more privacy and to hide your IP address. Remember the age old saying of not putting all your eggs in one basket? Well, the same thing applies with Bitcoins. Experts recommend separating your transactions into different wallets according to their importance, just like your bank accounts. Keep one wallet for daily transactions, one wallet for bigger expenditures, one for investments and so on.

Tip 2- Always Protect your identity

Always be careful of sharing information about your transactions in public spaces. This is to avoid revealing any information with regards to your personal ID with your Bitcoin address.

Tip 3- Use an Escrow Service

Using an escrow service acts as a middleman. When a buyer wishes to purchase a product or service online but isn't sure who is on the other side, they send their bitcoins to this escrow service while they wait to receive their item. On the other side, the seller receives confirmation that the money has been transacted but not yet remitted in the escrow service. The seller will then send the item to the buyer. When the buyer receives their merchandise, all they need to do is notify the escrow service to complete their payment.

Tip 4- Backup for your virtual wallets

Frequent updates are necessary to keep the security of your wallet in check. Just like any other backup policy, it is always good to back up your virtual information on a weekly basis, so no information is lost. When backing up your data, make sure to keep them encrypted.

Tip 5- Encrypt your Wallet too

Speaking of encryption, doing this to your wallet is also extremely crucial, especially if this wallet is stored online. Create a password with a variety of combinations such as- upper and lower case, numbers and symbols. DESlock+ is one such tool that you can use to encrypt your files and wallets that contain this sensitive information. If you can, encrypt your whole system or userspace where you store these sensitive files.

Tip 6- Use Two-Level Authentication

When sourcing for online storage services, always go for services that offer two-factor authentication as well as the use of hardware wallets. This is a crucial item to keep as an arsenal against malware and viruses and hacking because even service providers are vulnerable to hacking.

Tip 7- Avoid Using Wallets on Mobile Devices

Back when internet banking and online transactions were new to the app store, it was advised not to access your bank accounts through mobile apps. The same can be said for using Bitcoin wallets. Avoid using your mobile devices especially for transactions of large amounts of money. Because of the likelihood of the wallets being compromised or lost, it is always a good thing to keep your wallet on devices that aren't connected to the internet.

Tip 8- Use Multi-Signature Addresses

Using multi-signature addresses involves the use of more than one key and these keys are usually stored on separate equipment of authorized individuals. This is especially recommended for corporate transactions or transactions that require high levels of security. In the case of any hacking, the hacker would need to hack into multiple levels of equipment to be able to obtain these keys to steal the bitcoins. This no doubt makes hacking extremely hard and tiresome.

Tip 9- Update your networks

It is advised to regularly update and maintain your systems and networks used in your Bitcoin transactions. This advice goes even for online bank accounts. Update your security solutions and make sure you do regular scans for every network, system and operating software you use.

Tip 10- Get Rid of Access Virtual Tools

With Bitcoin, there are many apps, tools as well as the option for virtual wallets to be installed on your PC to help trade, buy and sell in the Bitcoin network. With each app or tool, there is an increased risk of security breach. Be sure to think carefully if you need to install all these tools on your PC or mobile device. If you are not using them as frequently as you think you are, then get rid of it. Virtual wallets are something most Bitcoin account holders do not need, but yet they are installed. If you are not using your virtual wallets, carefully remove it, so all hidden data and folders are completely destroyed. Take the extreme effort to locate any copies of data that may have been created and delete them.

Guaranteeing total protection of our online data and assets is impossible from hackers and digital thieves, however, knowing these tips can help you increase the security and be more aware of how you can further improve data protection.

Technology is open for everyone to use but protecting yourself online is an essential part of internet connectivity as well.

CHAPTER 5: HOW DOES BITCOIN MINING WORK?

By now, you should have an idea of how mining works in the Bitcoin system. Mining creates new bitcoins but the underlying purpose is to verify Bitcoin transactions, to keep up to date on the records of every transaction. It is also meant to secure the Bitcoin network from hackers and thieves.

To understand how mining works; we will look at two major components of Bitcoin:

Blockchain

Bitcoin is a new invention, and it is probably the most important invention in the 21st-century regarding the internet and digital currency. To understand Bitcoin mining is to know how the blockchain works and why it's considered a unique and defining factor in Bitcoin.

Although we did talk about the Blockchain in a previous chapter, we will discuss this again and see how it fits with mining.

The blockchain is created to record each and every single Bitcoin transactions that take place on the Bitcoin network. As previously mentioned, it serves as an open public ledger that allows everyone on the network to see what transactions have occurred.

When an individual downloads and installs Bitcoin onto their computer, the system also automatically downloads the block chain. The blockchain continually expands as more and more transactions take place all over the world. Because of the ever growing blockchain, the latest versions of the Bitcoin wallets do not contain the entire Blockchain.

There is absolutely no need or reason to download the entire blockchain. In fact, even hardcore Bitcoin users don't download the whole thing. Jake Smith, the author of Bitcoin News Roundup, advises that Bitcoin users should only plan to download the entire Bitcoin system if they plan on running mining or a node.

All Bitcoin clients have the same blockchain on their computers. Miners verify the address you are sending the coins to and confirm that it contains the recommended amount of bitcoins to complete a transaction. Jake Smith adds that while someone can create a transaction input and make it seem like they are sending you to say, five bitcoins when they actually have zero in their account, miners will reject this as soon as it goes through the mining stage because the system will detect that you have no BTC.

New transactions are added to the blockchain in blocks every 10 minutes. In a blockchain, there are two essential items. First, there is a list of every single transaction that has taken place all around the world in the last 10 minutes, and it comes with a code called a hash which includes the date of which block transactions came from. This is the 'chain' part of the blockchain.

Miners are responsible for taking these two pieces of information and condensing them into a new hash that fits a certain characteristic. This new hash must start with a certain number of zeros, and it will take up a significant computational power. The difficulty increases when more zeros are needed for every 2016 blocks added.

What the miners are doing is solving a complex problem to find the magic number with each increasing difficulty to make sure that the more computer power is added to the network, there will be only an average block time of around 10 minutes.

Hashes make it easier to compare transactions rather than keep track of individual transactions worldwide. Each has references of the hash that came before it. It reconfirms each single transaction again down the original 'genesis' block.

These hashes are much easier to compare rather than trying to keep track of every individual transaction in the world. And because each one references the hash that came before it, it revalidates every single transaction repeatedly down to the original "Genesis" block.

Risk & Rewards

Bitcoin is always under two likely problems. One, when traders try to spend and sell the exact Bitcoin twice and two, miners who try to include fake blocks into the system so they can receive new and valid bitcoins. Mining thus provides a secure way for the network to operate legally and away from all these problems.

Mining also minimizes the problem of 'double spending' because only one of two transactions will eventually make it into the blockchain. If both transactions are verified at first, miners will carry on validating these transactions. More and more blocks are added until either one wins out. Each block is confirmed at least six times, which takes about an hour before a trade is accepted. This is the reason why exchanges need to wait.

So what do minders get for validating transactions? They get 25 bitcoins whenever they successfully solve a block. This amount is cut in half once every four years or every 210,000 blocks.

How to Begin Mining?

Mining bitcoins requires a unique set of hardware. During the cryptocurrency infancy years, it was relatively easy to mine using personal computers, but that was only because the difficulty was low. But as more miners enter the Bitcoin network and computing technology continues to increase, the difficulty in solving blocks also increases to control the entry of new bitcoins.

The preferred method to mine Bitcoins is the ASIC mining method. The ASIC microchip is specially designed for solving hashing algorithms used by Bitcoin. Mining software used now are usually the free and open source. It connects users to the mining pools, running algorithms to solve hashes and deposits miner's earnings to their Bitcoin wallets.

Just as how the difficulty of mining has increased, the barrier of entry to become a miner is also high. Overhead costs for miners include special hardware as well at the electrical capacity needed to run it. To increase chances of solving a block first, miners must join mining pools. Here computational powers at separate locations are combined, and rewards are distributed among all the members in the mining pool. A minor cut of the reward is proportional to their percentage of the pool's total computing power. Mining without a pool is ineffective unless you have invested serious money into a house full of machinery.

Currently, there are two major mining pools in the Bitcoin market that make up close to half the market share. The pools are the GHash.IO and the Discus Fish. These pools account for more than 75% of all Bitcoin mining.

Each mining pool in the Bitcoin network is formed like a business. Miners have to abide by a set of guidelines, fees and agree to the methods of splitting rewards. The bigger the mining pool, the higher a miner's chances of getting a reward but the rewards are spread thinner among the members. At one time, each pool accommodates only one mining machine.

Solving A Block

To solve a block is a guessing game until you reach a solution that fits the equation. Solving a block is like a lottery. You play and play as many times as you can and want as quickly as your mining equipment can run.

It's difficult to predict how much money a miner can earn by mining bitcoins because there are so many variables such as the mining pool's membership as well as the pool's methods of divvying up rewards and not to mention hardware costs and performance and the cost of electricity.

There is a method though that can be used to get an estimate. Miners usually input details of their personal set up into Bitcoin Profitability Calculator and the Mining Hardware Comparison Table to get an idea of how much they would be making if they were to mine alone and calculate a system's hash rate.

A mining veterans advice for casual miners says it's good to invest in a few small ten gigabyte-hash miners such as the 10 GH/S Bitcoin Miner or the 11GH USB Stick Miner, each below USD300. If you want to become a serious miner, then be prepared to fork out at least USD2, 000 for an ASIC card or pre-made machines.

For example, if you spend USD1,000 on four 10GHps miners for a total hash rate of 40GHps. The profitability calculator estimates that a miner's return will be an average of 0.0012 bitcoins. This, of course, does not include hardware and electricity costs. Also, note that the difficulty increases, old hardware will be outdated, and returns of investment for a miner will also diminish. At present, there are over 13 million bitcoins in existence.

CHAPTER 6- THE FUTURE OF DIGITAL CURRENCY & BITCOIN

So what does the future of Bitcoin hold? Back in 2009 when Bitcoin came to life, not many noticed its existence except for a small group of programmers. The origins of Bitcoin is still pretty shadowy- is Satoshi Nakamoto really a person? Is it a group of individuals? Is it one individual? Two maybe? An amalgamation of names? Some secret Illuminati group?

Bitcoin, in its founding years, was set up as a cryptocurrency, where powerful encryption algorithms were manipulated to create a new way of enabling secure transactions. Records would be decentralized, users' identities would be privatized, and no one was in charge of Bitcoin.

Fast forward to 2016, Bitcoin now has about 14.6 million units in circulation with a collective market value of USD3.4 billion. The first few clients of Bitcoin were criminals who took advantage of the anonymity feature of Bitcoin but with rules and regulations put into place, Bitcoin has managed to draw the interest of top financial institutions such as JP Morgan and the New York Stock Exchange.

Through all of this, Bitcoin has been mocked by so many people and was believed to be doomed to die.

In 2009 when Bitcoin first came out, it has absolutely no value, even as 2010 rolled in. But by 2013, the boom of Bitcoin had arrived and by early 2014, it reached a high of USD 1216 million.

The Growing Up Years of Bitcoin

Bitcoin, is in all fairness, still in its infancy. Truth be told, its' survival is mainly due to the internet and the ever-growing access the whole world has to electricity and the World Wide Web. To date, Bitcoin is only seven years old. It's passed the threshold of a least the first five shaky years of growth and is steadily moving up fast.

Apart from the internet, millennials are also a contributing factor to the growth of Bitcoins. Millennials are more open and welcoming of new technology and ideas. They quickly adapt to disruptive technology and use it to make their lives better and faster.

Although Bitcoin is still in its infancy stages, investors are investing massive amounts of money into this cryptocurrency.

In 2014 to 2015, starting a Bitcoin company was one of the easiest ways to get funding. Despite the ease, investors were believed to be investing money into Bitcoin primary for greed, more than anything else.

Rectifying Problems

When Bitcoin first appeared it was filled with loopholes, inefficient companies, and very poor custodians- but the same can be said for all technologies and new start-ups.

Issues experienced by Mt.Gox, for instance, saw many individuals losing hundreds of millions of cash collectively.

Not only that, scandals such as the ones from Silk Road gave Bitcoin a poor standing amongst financial institutions and the average investor. People believed that Bitcoin was part of the black market and was only used for drugs and other illicit business.

But, Bitcoin grew, and its perception keeps on changing- for the better. Old exchanges are either gone or dying whereas the newer ones that came in, such as Coinbase, are fully loaded with security features and regulations to abide by.

Coinbase, for example, employs an armada of security analysts and tech individuals to work with regulators.

BitGo, for example, is another Bitcoin service provider that provides security software in the Bitcoin network for companies that cannot build or do not have their own funding to create secure platforms.

Growing Number of Users and Transactions

Companies such as Purse, ChangeTip, and ZapChain all offer various forms of Bitcoin technology to meet the demands of different types of transactions. Purse, for example, allows people to purchase goods on Amazon whereas ChangeTip offers users micro-transactions.

All these different service providers popping up on the Bitcoin network offer users and investors a variety of things to do in the Bitcoin marketplace. These services move Bitcoin up the financial game and offer different ways of spending, buying and investing in Bitcoins.

The Existential Crisis

According to the New York Times and Mike Hearn, Bitcoin is experiencing an existential crisis. This may or may not be true.

Bitcoin could be going through a growing pain as it continues to develop.

The Bitcoin community is asking for block sizes to increase but the Core development team has created a roadmap on how to scale Bitcoin and this includes the Segregated Witness implementation through the soft fork. Scaling is necessary- there is no denying this.

Bitcoin, at present, handles about three transactions per second and for Bitcoin to become a primary payment protocol on the internet, it needs to be able to support much more than this.

Another group of developers has created an alternative client for this Bitcoin protocol called Bitcoin Classic as they were not happy with the proposal put forth by the Core Development team.

This new proposal aims too hard fork a 2 MB block size which is double than what the current block size is. The good thing is, the majority of miners from BitMan, BitFury, and BW.com have all agreed to support this new hard fork feature. Not only that, the largest exchanges and wallets such as Coinbase, Xapo, and Blockchain.info all are on board with this new venture.

The question remains, should Bitcoin be a bigger competitor of payment options compared to Visa, Mastercard or Paypal? Or should Bitcoin remain as a settlement layer? Can Bitcoin maintain its status as a decentralized entity?

While Bitcoin may be going through an existential crisis, it is not a factor to believe the death of Bitcoin is near.

The Future of Bitcoin

All that can be said is the future of Bitcoin is bright, and it will get brighter. Joel Spolsky of JoelonSoftware.com says that it takes at least ten years to create useful software. Bitcoin is only now in its seventh year.

Jeff Garzik, the founder of Bloq, states " Bitcoin is comparable to the pre-web-browser 1992-era Internet. This is still the very early days of Bitcoin's life. The base layer protocol is now stable (TCP/IP). Now engineers are building the second layer (HTTP) that makes Bitcoin usable for average people and machines…"

People like Joel and Jeff believe that once the Bitcoin infrastructure is built and stable, it will no doubt pave the way for companies like Bloq, BitGo, and Coinbase to lead the way and see strong programs constructed in the application layer.

While this infrastructure is built, it is clear that Bitcoin itself keeps evolving.

The Future of Mining

While mining is centralized and concentrated to pools, companies like 21.co plan on changing this. On 21.co's company profile page, it states that "someone needs to build the full-stack infrastructure for Bitcoin, from silicon to software … that someone is us."

Pretty bold statement but one that 21.co is fully confident in achieving. Take for instance in November 2015; 21.co released its very first product- the 21 Bitcoin computers which are a dev kit to introduce developers to the glories of Bitcoin. 21.co continues to improve the dev kits design of the chips and it is very likely that they will roll out a router that can perpetually do a mining job continuously.

21.co also wants to create a mining software that can integrate a smaller minor version that can run on mobile devices. But before anyone gets excited, 21.co says that this program is not meant for individuals to get rich quick on the block reward. Rather the program's goal is for Bitcoin to become the energy to increase participation via the internet.

Say for example if you were to do a quick search on Google, you would need to go through ads and tracking cookies that follow your every move on the web. With 21.co's ideas, a developer can build a search engine over a 21 Bitcoin computer where all a user needs to do was pay a small tiny amount of Bitcoins to enable a search.

The core rationale here lays once you extract the idea of procuring bitcoins that sit within an individual user's wallet- this is what the idea of what the internet is and how it works begins to evolve.

So instead of companies taking an individual's browsing patterns or data, companies have to now pay a consumer for their data. Fred Wilson of Avc.com believes "Bitcoin finally finds a killer app with the emergence of Open Bazaar protocol powered zero take rate marketplaces."

Digital Gold

Bitcoin, unlike other investment tools and stocks, is very volatile now, but it isn't the only volatile asset in the world. Critics are quick to point out the 10% drop in the price of a very new asset but haven't the stock market experienced 10% drops in similar time frames? Look at oil for example or even coal and gold. These mature assets still experience price fluctuations. Many of the world's countries are reaping the benefits of digital gold. Countries like Argentina, Brazil, and India, have all experienced high points of volume through the use of Bitcoins. Even Russia, although they are considering making Bitcoin illegal so no doubters can see the growth of it in volumes.

Digital Currencies

While the future and survival of Bitcoin seem uncertain now, the technology driving it is sure to stay.

Bitcoin represents a radically new idea that the world still needs to understand and come to terms with. It is a radically new idea in the world of finance. Bitcoin uses a decentralized system for exchanging value, a concept most countries and central banks find hard to grasp as this may spell the reduce stronghold of power.

Despite being young technology, Bitcoin is an open-source and copyright free core program, making it easy to develop continuously and improve to create more functional and desirable cryptocurrencies.

Programmers all across the globe have all started to develop military-grade encryptions to introduce new ways of trading which in time, brings about a stabilizing fixture to prices.

Over time, you can see that all these kinks and wrinkles in the future of Bitcoins are being smoothed out.

Digital currencies exist mainly as entries into accounting software and systems. This system just acts as a public ledger viewable by all that records transactions among addresses.

Owning digital currency isn't the same as having actual real money in your pocket. What it means is that you have your own personal claim to a specific address with your own password and the right to do whatever you want with it, especially without any other figures telling you how to deal with your address. This clever system of digital currencies will continue to disrupt traditional and global currencies.

Digital Payments

Online transactions will continue to grow with more and more businesses opening up options for transacting in digital currencies. If you want to make a purchase online, all you needed to do is pay for it with your digital currencies. If you do not have any digital currencies, then you can buy some online from an online exchange and 'send' it to your digital wallet.

Using your smartphone app, you just switch the app on when it's time to pay. A specific biometric is used to unlock your address. The currency network then publicly informs that you have transferred $100 digital currency to your store.

This all happens in a matter of milliseconds with almost no fees, or personal information included in the transaction.

Your credit or debit card transactions take nearly three days to confirm and with it, your sensitive personal information is given to confirm the conventional transaction.

Other Forms of Virtual Currencies

Bitcoin isn't the only digital currency in the world. However, it is the most popular and successful digital currency to date. Currently, there are over 150 digital currencies available. Apart from Bitcoin, here is another two other types of digital currencies creating waves in the cryptocurrency world:

Litecoin:

Created by former Google engineer Charlie Lee, Litecoin is the second largest cryptocurrency in the world. Litecoin is also open-source and decentralized.

Darkcoin (DASH):

Darkcoin is a secret version of Bitcoin. Darkcoin aims to make transactions even more anonymous than Bitcoin. Bitcoin stores its transactions in a public ledger, and this ledger can reveal a lot of information when you look closely. Darkcoin, on the other hand, works on a master code network that makes all transactions virtually untraceable. Since its launch in January 2014, Darkcoin has managed to gather a large following.

The Bitcoin Reality

Bitcoin has many years ahead of it for exponential growth. While it may not be perfect and have loads of problems to overcome, it isn't dead. Most of the world's biggest critics for Bitcoins are the ones whose income continues to come from conventional means of payment. For them to label it dead or call for it to be banned or replaced is, of course, naïve and shortsighted.

Bitcoin will no doubt become the Internet's first and real payment protocol.

As the years go by and internet technology increases, new applications will be built and be used in Bitcoin. To understand Bitcoin's true potential, we need to look forward into the decades ahead, not just upcoming years.

Fortunately for miners, users and investors- the future of Bitcoin are on the right track.

Conclusion

Thank you again for downloading this book!

I hope this book was able to help you to gain more knowledge about the world of Bitcoin, what it is, where it's going, how it benefits us and the possible dangers it presents. Not everyone is a tech-savvy individual, which is why this book was intentionally created in an easily digestible format, free of jargon and complex concepts.

Now that you've been exposed to the information in this book, the next step is to apply the knowledge you gained to your life however you can. Whether you want to trade Bitcoins or invest or simply use it as a form of payments, the possibilities with Bitcoin are endless.

As illustrated in this book, using Bitcoin is crucial to stay current and keep up with technology. While many believe that Bitcoin is in a position to replace conventional currencies, it's possible that the two will join forces rather than remain opposites. It is my hope that this book provided relevant and valuable information for you that you can apply to your own life.

Printed in Great Britain
by Amazon